How Toys Work

Pulleys

Siân Smith

www.raintreepublishers.co.uk
Visit our website to find out
more information about
Raintree books.

To order:
☎ Phone 0845 6044371
▤ Fax +44 (0) 1865 312263
▣ Email myorders@raintreepublishers.co.uk

Customers from outside the UK please telephone +44 1865 312262

Raintree is an imprint of Capstone Global Library Limited,
a company incorporated in England and Wales having its
registered office at 7 Pilgrim Street, London, EC4V 6LB
– Registered company number: 6695582

Text © Capstone Global Library Limited 2013
First published in hardback in 2013
First published in paperback in 2014
The moral rights of the proprietor have been asserted.

Edited by Dan Nunn, Rebecca Rissman, and Sian Smith
Designed by Joanna Hinton-Malivoire
Picture research by Mica Brancic
Production by Victoria Fitzgerald
Originated by Capstone Global Library Ltd
Printed in China

ISBN 978 1 4062 3799 3 (hardback)
16 15 14 13 12
10 9 8 7 6 5 4 3 2 1

ISBN 978 1 4062 3806 8 (paperback)
17 16 15 14 13
10 9 8 7 6 5 4 3 2 1

British Library Cataloguing in Publication Data
Smith, Sian.
    Pulleys. -- (How toys work)
    1. Pulleys--Juvenile literature.
    I. Title II. Series
    621.8′5-dc22

Acknowledgements
The author and publisher are grateful to the following for permission
to reproduce copyright material: © Capstone Global Library Ltd pp.5,
6, 7, 8, 9, 11, 22b, 23 bottom (Karon Dubke), 12, 13, 14, 15, 18,
19, 20, 21, 23 top (Lord and Leverett), 16, 17 (Tudor Photography);
Shutterstock pp.4 top left (© Galchenkova Ludmila), 4 bottom right
(© Gorilla), 4 top right (© Hirurg), 4 bottom left (© Ron Zmiri), 10 (©
Alberto Tirado), 22a (© Cheryl Casey), 22c (© bluecrayola), 22d (©
Dikiiy).

Cover photograph of a boy on a zip line reproduced with permission
of Corbis (© moodboard). Back cover photograph of a toy crane
reproduced with permission of © Capstone Publishers (Karon Dubke).

We would like to thank David Harrison, Nancy Harris, Dee Reid, and
Diana Bentley for their assistance in the preparation of this book.

Every effort has been made to contact copyright holders of material
reproduced in this book. Any omissions will be rectified in subsequent
printings if notice is given to the publisher.

Contents

Different toys 4

Pulleys .6

Joining pulleys. 12

More toys with pulleys 16

Quiz 22

Picture glossary 23

Index 24

Different toys

There are many different kinds of toys.

Toys work in different ways.

Pulleys

pulley

Some toys use pulleys.

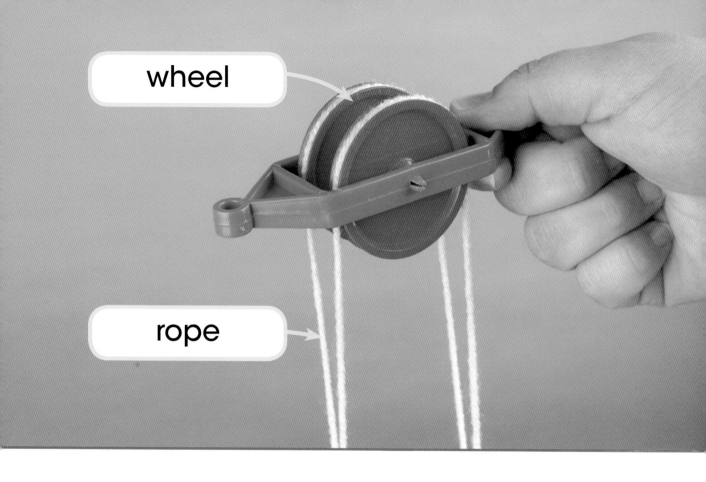

wheel

rope

A pulley is a wheel with a rope around it.

You can pull one end of the rope to lift something up.

You can let go of the rope to move
something down.

pulley

A pulley can help us to lift heavy things.

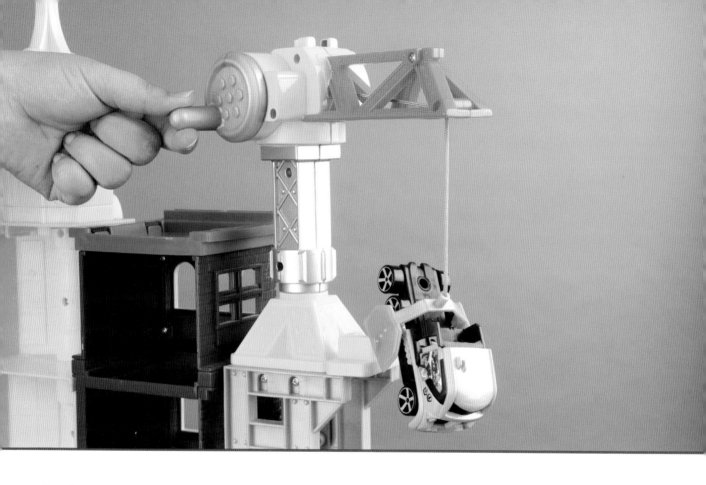

A toy crane uses a pulley to
lift things.

Joining pulleys

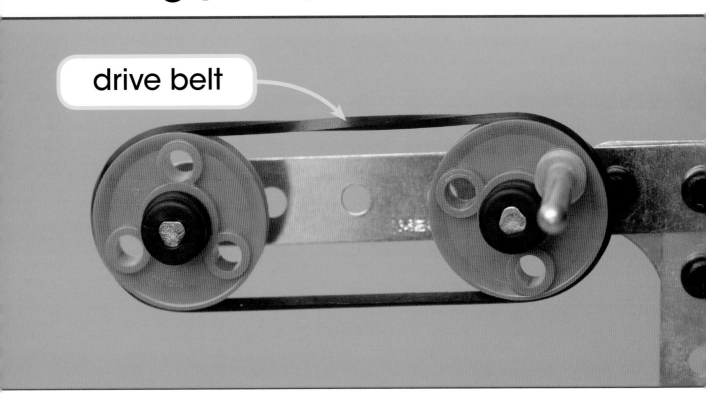

drive belt

You can join two pulleys with a drive belt.

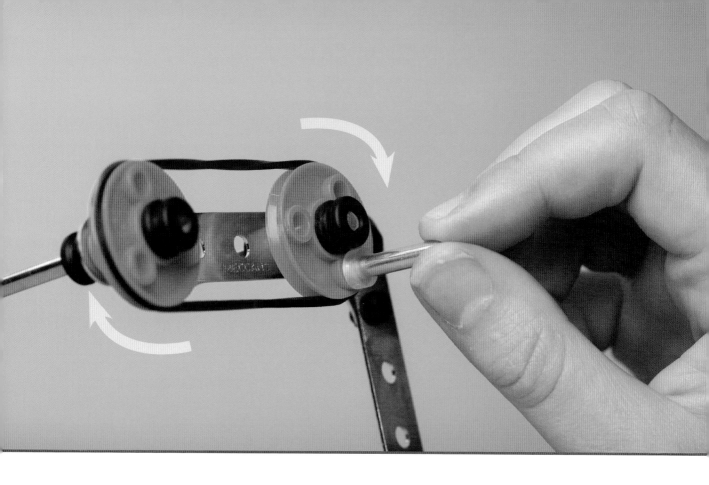

When you turn one pulley, the other turns too.

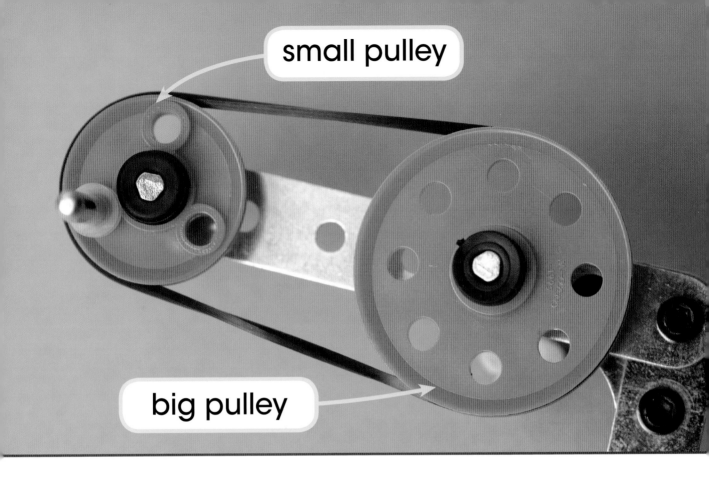

small pulley

big pulley

A big pulley and a small pulley can
be joined together.

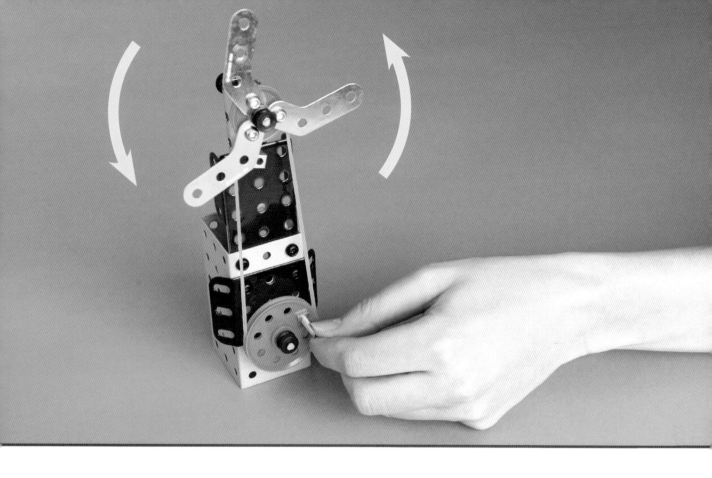

It is harder to push the big pulley.

But it makes the small pulley turn fast.

More toys with pulleys

pulley

This toy roller coaster works with
a pulley.

The pulley takes the carts up to
the top.

pulley

This toy boat works with a pulley.

lifeboat

The pulley lifts lifeboats up
and down.

pulley

This toy truck works with a pulley.

The pulley lifts cars up and down.

Quiz

(a)

(b)

(c)

(d)

Which one of these toys uses a pulley to work?

Answer on page 24

Picture glossary

 **drive belt** a band that wraps around two wheels. It joins the wheels so that when one wheel turns, the other does too.

 **pulley** a wheel with a rope around it. We use pulleys to help us lift things up or put them down.

Index

boat 18, 19

car 21

crane 11

drive belt 12–15

push 15

roller coaster 16, 17

Answer to question on page 22: Toy b uses a pulley to work.

Notes for parents and teachers

Introduction

Show the children a collection of toys. One or more of the toys should have a pulley mechanism. Ask the children if they can spot the toy with the pulley. Alternatively show the children pictures of pulleys, for example those used on a flagpole, a boat, and a crane. Do they know what a pulley is and what it does?

More information about pulleys

Explain that a pulley is a wheel with a rope, chain, or belt wrapped around it. Show the children an example of a grooved pulley wheel and explain that many pulleys have a dip or groove around the edge of the wheel to stop the rope, chain, or belt from slipping off the sides. A pulley is a simple machine that helps us to lift things up or lower them down. Pulleys also make it easier for us to lift or move heavy things.

Follow up activities

Support the children in using a construction set to create a working pulley. For example, you could make a simple crane and use this to lift something, or make a windmill similar to the one on page 15. For more advanced work on simple machines, children can work with an adult to discuss and play the games at: www.edheads.org/activities/simple-machines